There's a lovely little poem by Noël Coward which I had quite forgotten until Patricia Hodge kindly reminded me of it:

When I have fears, as Keats had fears,
Of the moment I'll cease to be,
I console myself with vanished years,
Remembered laughter, remembered tears,
And the peace of the changing sea.

When I feel sad, as Keats felt sad,
That my life is nearly done,
It gives me comfort to dwell upon
Remembered friends who are dead and gone
And the jokes we had, and the fun.

How happy they are I cannot know,
But happy am I who loved them so.

In all the years I have been collecting, I don't believe that I have ever touched on the subject of campanology. But how about this passage, which comes from the old Dorothy Sayers detective story, The Nine Tailors:

The eight men advanced to their stations, and Hezekiah consulted his watch. "Time!" he said. He spat upon his hands, grasped the sallie of Tailor Paul, and gently swung the great bell over the balance. Toll-toll-toll; and a pause; toll-toll-toll; and a pause; toll-toll-toll; the nine tailors, or teller-strokes, that mark the passing of a man. The year is dead; toll him out with twelve strokes more, one for every passing month. Then silence. Then, from the faint, sweet, tubular chimes of the clock overhead, the four quarters and the twelve strokes of midnight. The ringers grasped their ropes. "Go!" The bells give tongue: Gaude, Sabaoth, John, Jericho, Jubilee, Dimity, Batty Thomas and Tailor Paul, rioting and exalting far up in the dark tower, wide mouths rising and falling, brazen tongues clamouring, huge wheels turning to the dance of the leaping ropes. Tin tan din dan bim bam bom bom tan tin din dan bam bim bo bom – tin tan dan din bim bam bom bo – tan tin dan din bam bim bo bom – tan dan tin bam din bo bim bom – every bell in her place striking tuneably, hunting up, hunting down, dodging, snapping, laying her blows behind, making her thirds and fourths, working down to lead the dance again. Out over the flat, white wastes of fen, over the spear-straight, steel-dark dykes and the wind-bent, groaning poplar trees, bursting from the snow-choked louvres of the belfry, whirled away southward and westward in gusty blasts of clamour to the sleeping counties went the music of the bells – little Gaude, silver Sabaoth, strong John and Jericho, sweet Dimity and old Batty Thomas, with great Tailor Paul bawling and striding like a giant in the midst of them. Up and down went the shadows of the ringers upon the walls, up and down went the scarlet sallies flickering roofwards and floorwards, and up and down, hunting in their courses, went the bells of Fenchurch St Paul.

At Easter 1949 the Boy Scouts instituted what was known as "Bob a Job" week – "bob" being the slang word for a shilling just as "quid" was (and is) for a pound. In late October 2011 – I stupidly failed to note the exact date – Mr George Reid of Edinburgh wrote to The Times:

Sir,

My late sister-in-law, a Girl Guide commissioner, was just in time to persuade a group of the unwisdom of their proposed effort to compete with the local Scouts. The title they had in mind was "willing for a shilling".

Ann Thwaite has called my attention to a nice story told by Roy Jenkins in his "Lives of the Chancellors". It concerns Sir John Simon, formerly both Chancellor of the Exchequer and Lord Chancellor, and the Oxford left-wing economist G.D.H. Cole:

Returning from a weekend [at All Souls] on a Monday morning, Simon encountered Cole on the platform of Oxford station and greeted him with his well-known false bonhomie. As the London train came in Cole, disapproving of Simon and eager to make a display of semi-proletarianism as well as to escape, said "I must get along to my third-class compartment" and disappeared down the platform. Simon, determined not to be frustrated in his search for ecumenical companionship, announced that he always travelled "third" himself and loped after him. In those days railway tickets were neat little cardboard rectangles about two inches by one, first-class ones virginally white, third-class ones more earthily green. When the ticket-collector came round they both, with varying degrees of embarrassment, produced white tickets.

A few magical lines from The Waste Land*:*

> A woman drew her long black hair out tight
> And fiddled whisper music on those strings
> And bats with baby faces in the violet light
> Whistled, and beat their wings
> And crawled head downward down a blackened wall
> And upside down in air were towers
> Tolling reminiscent bells, that kept the hours
> And voices singing out of empty cisterns and exhausted wells.

Hugh Latimer (1487-1555) was Bishop of Worcester before the Reformation, and later Church of England chaplain to King Edward VI. He was burnt at the stake by Bloody Mary. Here is an extract from one of his Christmas sermons.

To show themselves obedient, came Joseph and Mary unto Bethlehem; a long journey, and poor folks, and peradventure on foot; for we read of no great horses that she had, as our great ladies have nowadays; for truly she had no such jolly gear...

Well, she was great with child, and was now come to Bethlehem, where they could get never a lodging in no inn, and so were compelled to lie in a stable; and there Mary, the mother of Christ, brought forth that blessed child... and there "she wrapped Him in swaddling clothes and laid Him in a manger, because there was no room for them at the inn." For the innkeepers took only those who were able to pay for their good cheer; they would not meddle with such beggarly folk as Joseph and Mary his wife were...

But I warrant you, there was many a jolly damsel at that time in Bethlehem, yet amongst them all there was not one found that would humble herself so much as once to go and see poor Mary in the stable, and to comfort her. No, no; they were too fine to take so much pains, I warrant you, they had bracelets and vardingales; like as there be many nowadays amongst us, which study nothing else but how they may desire fine raiment; and in the mean season they suffer poor Mary to lie in the stable...

But what was her swaddling-clothes wherein she laid the King of heaven and earth? No doubt it was poor gear; peradventure it was her kercher which she took from her head, or such like gear; for I think Mary had not much fine linen; she was not trimmed up as our women be nowadays; for in the old time women were content with honest and single garments. Now they have found out these round-a-bouts; they were not invented then; the devil was not so cunning to make such gear, he found it out afterward.

Here is a question to be moved. Who fetched water to wash the child after it was born into the world, and who made a fire? It is like that Joseph did such things; for, as I told you before, those fine damsels thought it scorn to do any such thing unto Mary.

But, I pray you, to whom was the Nativity of Christ first opened? To the bishops, or great lords which were at that time at Bethlehem? Or to those jolly damsels with their vardingales, with their round-a-bouts, or with their bracelets? No, no: they had so many lets to trim and dress themselves, that they could have no time to hear of the Nativity of Christ.

But his nativity was narrated first to the shepherds...

I have my friend Jon Halliday to thank for this treasure:

In 1955, having buried the idea of a Stalin museum, Khrushchev decided that his dacha would be transferred to the Central Committee to serve as an isolated location where groups of Central Committee employees could get together to propose various reports and analyses for the Politburo. They then began to refurnish the building for this purpose. Much of Stalin's furniture was removed and taken to the vast underground chambers that had been built before and during the war as air raid shelters. Aleksei Snegov, an acquaintance of ours who had been an aide to Khrushchev, told me that when Stalin's desk was being moved from his former study, they accidentally came across five letters addressed to him that he had hidden under a layer of newspapers in one of the drawers. Snegov could only recall three of them. One had been dictated by Lenin on 5 March 1923. He demanded that Stalin apologize for his abusive manner towards Krupskaya [Lenin's wife]... The second letter was from Bukharin, awaiting death, written shortly before he was shot. He finished with the words: "Koba, why do you need my death?" The third came from Marshal Tito in 1950. The text was brief: "Stalin, stop sending assassins to murder me. We have already caught five, one with a bomb, another with a rifle... If this doesn't stop, I will send one man to Moscow and there will be no need to send another."

Z.A. and R.A. Medvedev
Stalin's Personal Archive: hidden or destroyed? Facts and Theories

When the Duke of Medina Sidonia was appointed by King Philip II to the command of the Spanish Armada, he replied as follows:

My health is not equal to such a voyage, for I know by experience of the little I have been at sea that I am always seasick and always catch cold. My family is burdened with a debt of nine hundred thousand ducats, and I could not spend a rial in the King's service. Since I have had no experience either of the sea or of war, I cannot feel that I ought to command so important an enterprise. I know nothing of what the Marquis of Santa Cruz has been doing, or of what intelligence he has of England, so that I feel I should give but a bad account of myself, commanding thus blindly, and being obliged to rely on the advice of others, without knowing good from bad, or which of my advisers might want to deceive or displace me. The Adelantado Major of Castile is much fitter for this post than I. He is a man of much experience in military and naval matters, and a good Christian too.

As Garrett Mattingley writes, "this is not exactly the spirit that conquered Mexico and Peru." The poor Duke got the job anyway; the royal secretaries confessed that they had not dared show his letter to the King.

The following was sent me by my friend John Woolley:

God Wants to Know

God would like to thank you for your belief and patronage. In order better to sense your needs, He asks that you take a few moments to answer the following questions. Please keep in mind that your responses will be kept completely confidential and that you need not disclose your name or address unless you desire a direct response to your comments or suggestions.

1. How did *you* first hear about God?

   □ newspaper   □ divine inspiration
   □ television   □ other
   □ word of mouth

2. Are you currently using any other sources of information, security or guidance, in addition to God? Please tick all that apply.

   □ none   □ biorhythmics   □ sex
   □ tarot   □ insurance policies   □ alcohol
   □ fortune cookies   □ lottery   □ other
   □ horoscopes   □ television
   □ self-help books   □ advice columns

3. God generally employs a limited amount of Divine Intervention to keep a balanced level of felt presence and blind faith. Would you prefer (circle one)

   A. more Divine Intervention
   B. less Divine Intervention
   C. current level of Divine Intervention just right
   D. don't know

4. God also attempts to maintain a fairly balanced level of disasters and miracles. Please rate on a scale of 1-5 His handling of the following:

   a. disasters (flood, famine, war)   b. miracles (recovery from disease, heroic rescues, sports upsets)

   1. unsatisfactory   1. unsatisfactory
   2. poor   2. poor
   3. average   3. average
   4. good   4. good
   5. excellent   5. excellent

5. Do you have any additional comments or suggestions for improving the quality of God's services?

Thank you

I have been reading the excellent biography of the musician Constant Lambert by Stephen Lloyd. He quotes a splendid passage from a radio talk by Lambert on his old friend, that most eccentric of dilettante composers, Lord Berners:

Although the best of hosts, and nothing could have been gayer than his weekends when company, cuisine and conversation were all at an equally high level, he was at heart a rather shy and nervous man given, like most famous wits, to bouts of melancholia and quite wrongly distrustful of his own abilities. A typical example of his desire for solitude combined with his own individual humour was provided by his simple method of keeping a railway carriage to himself. Instead of employing the usual English tactics he would put on dark glasses and slyly beckon in the passers-by. Those isolated figures who took the risk of entering the carriage became so perturbed by his habit of reading the newspaper upside down and taking his temperature every few minutes that they invariably changed carriages at the next station.

My dear first wife Anne picked up from Sue Prideaux's superb biography of Strindberg some startling information on the funeral of Victor Hugo:

Hugo was given a state funeral, but his will stipulated that he should be sent to his grave in a pauper's coffin. Down through a sea of mourners rolled the humble ship of state, saluted at the Arc de Triomphe by a guard of young poets, and down the Champs-Elysées by the whores of Paris, who had decided to honour the dead man by offering their services free in the broad margins of that great thoroughfare.

My pen-friend David Langford produces a monthly pamphlet called **Ansible**, *which always includes a section on excruciatingly awful writing. Here are a few examples:*

General Vigo, a tall snowy-haired albino from Urinal, fourth satellite moon of Saturn.

Bengo Mistral, *Pirates of Cerebus*, 1953

The question hung there, like an invisible cloud of flatulence.

Neal Stephenson, *Reamde*, 2011

He picked up his coat from the back of the sofa, and moved to the door, feeling distinctly like an ambulant and green soft fruit.

Keith McCarthy, *The Silent Sleep of the Dying*, 2004

She met Prabhat's gaze. This modern day Brahman wouldn't cow her.

Sarah K. Castle, *The Information in a Dream*, 2012

Her supple arms drooped to the floor and encircled the lamp overhead. Then her long legs joined in.

Paul Kohout, *The Widow Killer*, 1998

"The Reason is a girl. I'm a poor man, and she's heiress to fabulous – well, frankly, she's the daughter of 3W28W12 himself."

Paul Ernst, *The Planetoid of Peril*, 1931

Lord Beaverbrook, press baron par excellence, founder of the Daily Express *and inspiration for Evelyn Waugh's Lord Copper – he happens also to have been my godfather – was the son of a Scottish-born Presbyterian minister who made his home in New Brunswick. At the drop of a hat he would recite his favourite poem:*

> I know that God is wrath with me
> For I was born in sin;
> My heart is so exceeding vile
> No virtue dwells therein.
> Awake I sin, asleep I sin,
> I sin with every breath;
> When Adam fell he went to hell
> And damned us all to death – beautiful, isn't it?

My mother did a wonderful imitation.

In early September 1959 I received a letter from my old chum Philip Ziegler. We were both in the Foreign Service; Philip was in Vientiane, I was in Beirut. The letter ran as follows:

My dear John Julius,

On Sept. 11 or so a great, grotesque lobster will trip and fall heavily from a plane at Beirut aerodrome. It will wear a monocle and, probably, a kilt. It will be called Alec Brodie, will have a D.S.O. and an M.C., and will be the ex-Military Attaché in Laos and the new one in the Lebanon.

Alec first arrived in my life about three weeks before the War Office condescended to let us know that our pleas to be spared an M.A. because we had nowhere to put him were to be ignored. He telegraphed from Seoul: "To the Assistant Military Attaché: Will be glad to take over any stores left by former M.A. But do not like Ballantyne's whisky. Brodie." This took us aback, but we worked out who he must be and the correspondence began to work up speed. "Following for Brodie: There has been no M.A. Consequently there is no A.M.A. and no whisky. When do you arrive?" "To the A.M.A.: Then I will bring my own whisky. Did the M.A. have a dog which I should take on? Brodie." "There was no M.A. Consequently no A.M.A. and no dog. When do you arrive?" "To the A.M.A.: I am glad the M.A. had no dog. I do not like dogs. Should I bring a) tent; b) jeep; c) chauffeur; d) clerk; e) officer's servant; f) canvas bucket? Brodie." "There is no A.M.A. Tent, jeep and canvas bucket will all be useful. Advise against a) chauffeur, b) clerk and c) officer's servant since there is nowhere for them to live except a) tent, b) jeep and c) canvas bucket." "To the A.M.A.: Thank you. What about rope?" This was ignored and for fourteen blissful days we tried to kid ourselves that it was all a bad dream. Then: "To the A.M.A.: Arrive noon tomorrow. Chauffeur, clerk, jeep, officer's servant, tent and canvas bucket follow by road. Brodie."

Tomorrow was today by the time we got the telegram and even before the news had sunk in he was upon us, in a lorry commandeered from somewhere, with six cases of whisky, fourteen cases of beer and one very small suitcase, all flown up overweight at the expense of the War Office.

I commend Alec to you heartily, tho' with certain reservations. If you ask him to dinner he will destroy – not just break: crush, annihilate – your coffee-cups, spill wine on your table and cigar-ash on your carpet, go to sleep after dinner, wake up with a start at ten o'clock and proceed to lecture the most Lebanese of your guests in execrable but determined French on the genealogies of the greater Scottish families. I have heard him talk for half an hour without stop on the ramifications of the Frasers to a Laotian captain who had once been to France on a course and had a vague impression that Scotland was somewhere in America. But for all this his goodwill and kindness are immense, his patience and tolerance inexhaustible, he has the most unexpected and charming humility and, if the Lebanese have anything at all in common with the Laotians or Koreans, they will love him.

Be kind to him. Love, Philip.

P.S. Despite his medals and great gallantry, his many wounds are all self-inflicted. Never drive with him if you can avoid it.

James Baker Pyne was born in Bristol in 1800 and died in London in 1870.
He was a follower of Turner, and an extremely good painter. Siegfried Sassoon
wrote of him:

> For J.B. Pyne Victorian clumps of trees
> Were golden in a bland October breeze;
> Large clouds, like safe investments, loitered by,
> And distant Dartmoor loomed in sombre blue.

Has there ever been a more striking simile than that in line 3?

The Rev. Lord William Cecil was the second son of the Prime Minister Lord Salisbury. Born in 1863, in 1916 he became Bishop of Exeter, where he remained until his death in 1936. There he gained a reputation for eccentricity, thanks to which he was nicknamed "Love in a Mist". When travelling around his diocese (frequently by bicycle) he would often telephone his wife to ask where he was.

He kept an excellent chef and a splendid cellar; invitations to the Bishop's Palace were consequently much sought after by Exeter society. The story is told of how at one of his dinner parties the lady sitting next to him saw that she was being passed over by the butler as he served the wine. The following conversation ensued:

"Excuse me, Bishop, but I wonder if I could have a little of your delicious wine? Your butler seems to have forgotten me."

"My dear lady, you must forgive me. Of course – Johnson, please pour my guest some wine at once. But I fear I have a confession to make: I did in fact give orders that you were not to be given wine, since I understood that you were the President of the Temperance League."

"Oh no, Bishop, you are quite mistaken. I am the President of the Chastity League."

"Oh dear, I'm so sorry. I knew there was something you didn't do."

General Freiherr Kurt von Hammerstein-Equord (1878-1943) was Chief of the German High Command. He supervised the manual on the Military Unit Command (Truppenführung), which was published in October 1933. Here is an extract.

I divide my officers into four classes; the clever, the lazy, the industrious and the stupid. Each officer possesses at least two of these qualities. Those who are clever and industrious I appoint to the General Staff. Use can be made in certain circumstances of those who are stupid and lazy. The man who is clever and lazy qualifies for the highest command. He has the requisite nerves and the mental clarity to deal with all situations. But whoever is stupid and industrious must be got rid of, for he is too dangerous.

Some interesting historical facts:

Addison composed walking to and fro in a large room, a bottle of wine at each end. Barham [Ingoldsby Legends] had a cat on each shoulder. Dumas *aîné* wrote novels on blue paper, articles on pink, poetry on yellow, and wouldn't use same pen for novel and play. He received Wagner dressed in plumed helmet, lifebelt and flowered Japanese dressing-gown – and put on woollen socks for love scenes. Conrad wrote every book six times; P. Oppenheim used to dictate three books at once, Handel always composed in court dress, and Emerson wrote his essay on M. Angelo in a coat he had bought in Florence.

Leonard Alston

I found this in George Lyttelton's Commonplace Book. Just below is, unattributed, another interesting fact:

Sixteen kisses are mentioned in Jane Austen's novels, not one exchanged by a pair of lovers. Sex never intrudes.

From the same source, here is Harold Laski on Virginia Woolf:

It was like seeing someone organise his own immortality. Every phrase and gesture was studied. Now and again when she had said something a little out of the ordinary she wrote it down herself in a notebook.

There are also three miscellaneous entries:

Arnold Bennett and James Agate agreed that *"Voglio la mia colazione"* sung is all right, but not "I want my breakfast".

Better the cold blast of winter than the hot breath of a pursuing elephant.

Chinese proverb

Wilfrid Blunt's idea of heaven was to be laid to sleep in a garden with running water near for 100,000 years, then to be woken by a bird singing and to call out the person one loved best "Are you there?" "Yes, are you?" then turn round and go to sleep for another 100,000 years. Alfred Austin's was also to sit in a garden and to receive constant telegrams announcing alternately a British victory by sea and a British victory by land.

From my friend Dr Richard Shepherd of York comes the following, from "Lolly Willowes" by Sylvia Townsend Warner:

Henry Penny was the organist. He had lost one leg and three fingers in a bus accident, so there was scarcely any other profession he could have taken up.

Thomas Traherne lived from 1636 to 1674, but was unknown until the winter of 1896-7, when two manuscript volumes of his poems were discovered by chance in a street bookstall. His "Centuries of Meditations", which includes the following extraordinary passage, was first published in 1908.

The corn was orient and immortal wheat, which never should be reaped, nor was ever sown. I thought it had stood from everlasting to everlasting. The dust and stones of the street were as precious as gold; the gates were at first the end of the world. The green trees when I saw them first through one of the gates transported and ravished me, their sweetness and unusual beauty made my heart to leap, and almost mad with ecstasy, they were such strange and wonderful things: The Men! O what venerable and reverend creatures did the aged seem! Immortal Cherubims! And young men glittering and sparkling Angels, and maids strange seraphic pieces of life and beauty! Boys and girls tumbling in the street, and playing, were moving jewels. I knew not that they were born or should die; but all things abided eternally as they were in their proper places. Eternity was manifest in the Light of the Day; and something infinite behind everything appeared which talked with my expectation and moved my desire. The city seemed to stand in Eden, or to be built in Heaven. The streets were mine, the temple was mine, the people were mine, their clothes and gold and silver were mine, as much as their sparkling eyes, fair skins and ruddy faces. The skies were mine, and so were the sun and moon and stars, and all the World was mine; and I the only spectator and enjoyer of it. I knew no churlish proprieties, nor bounds, nor divisions; but all proprieties and divisions were mine; all treasures and the possessors of them. So that with much ado I was corrupted, and made to learn the dirty devices of this world. Which I now unlearn, and become, as it were, a little child again that I may enter into the Kingdom of God.

Traherne's work has been described as "bafflingly simple" – which just about sums it up.

We ate our breakfast lying on our backs
Because the shells were bursting overhead.
I bet a rasher to a loaf of bread
That Hull United would beat Halifax
When Jimmy Strainthorpe played full-back instead
Of Billy Bradford. Ginger raised his head
And cursed, and took the bet; and dropped back dead.
We ate our breakfast lying on our backs
Because the shells were bursting overhead.

Wilfred Gibson

A wartime advertisement for "Chappie" dog food:

If your dog is deprived of "Chappie", just tell him how sorry we are. Give him this message from his more fortunate brothers: "Cheer up old chap, we know the good things you are missing. Bark for the downfall of Hitler. Then, when peace comes, see that your master puts you on "Chappie". We'll say it's worth barking for!.

The late Professor Owen Chadwick wrote a perfectly fascinating short book called "Britain and the Vatican during the Second World War". Not surprisingly, a large part in it was played by Sir D'Arcy Osborne, British Minister to the Holy See from 1936 to 1947. Sir D'Arcy was thus a prisoner in the Vatican throughout the entire war, during which he was one of a group which – supported largely by his own money – helped to conceal some 4,000 escapees, both Jews and Allied soldiers, from the Nazis. I remember him well.

His dressing-gown was of camel's hair, and he wore a George IV sovereign on his key-chain. He hated hats, especially the black hats affected by Anthony Eden and called by the name of that statesman. He hated wearing uniform and felt like a page-boy when correctly dressed as an ambassador. He refused even to wear waistcoats. He liked pigskin, and caviare, and oysters, and Sheraton furniture, and expensive footwear. He disliked women who wore trousers. He had a touch of the introspective. People who saw him out for a solitary walk could fancy him rapt in deep thought. Certainly he was amusedly self-critical. He was amused to have his fortune told, and was interested in telepathy, and quarter-hoped that astrology might have something in it. He would have liked to believe in witches and the god Pan, though he confessed the Vatican was not the likeliest place to see a witch sail by on a broomstick. With only a half-sceptical smile he wore a charm against cosmic rays.

In 1963, Sir D'Arcy was somewhat surprised to succeed his second cousin once removed as Duke of Leeds. He died a year later, and the dukedom died with him. He is quoted by Professor Chadwick as having written in his diary:

I reached the grave conclusion during the Mass that I am nothing but a pencilled marginal note in the Book of Life. I am not in the main text at all.

Hitler played cricket, but only once. In 1930 it was claimed that, having seen British prisoners of war playing in southern Germany during the First World War, the Nazi party leader asked to be "initiated into the mysteries of our national game." A match was played against Hitler's XI, after which he declared that the rules should be altered by the "withdrawal of the use of pads" and using a "bigger and harder ball."

Ben Macintyre
Double Cross: The True Story of the D-Day Spies.